Sylvain and Jocosa

Retold by
Kelly Morrow

Printed with support from the Waldorf Curriculum Fund

Published by:
Waldorf Publications at the
Research Institute for Waldorf Education
38 Main Street
Chatham, NY 12037

Title: *Sylvain and Jocosa*
Author and Illustrator: Kelly Morrow
Editor: David Mitchell
Proofreader: Ann Erwin
Cover: David Mitchell
Cover Art: Kelly Morrow
© 2010 by AWSNA
ISBN #978-1-936367-03-0
Printed by McNaughton & Gunn
Saline, MI 48176 USA
June 2010

Second printing 2014
CreateSpace On-Demand Publishing

Chapter I

Once upon a time there lived two children who were best of friends. They lived in the same village. One was named Sylvain and the other Jocosa. Both were known for their beauty, kindness and wisdom. However, it happened to be that their

parents were not on terms of friendship with one another. This was due to some quarrel, which had taken place so long ago that they had forgotten what it was all about. But, still, they kept up the feud from habit.

This did not seem to affect Sylvain and Jocosa who were never happy when they were apart. Day after day, they fed their flocks of sheep together. They spent the long sunny hours of the afternoon playing in the fields or resting upon some shady hillside.

One day, the Fairy of the Meadows passed by and saw the two children. She was drawn to their gentle manners and radiant beauty.

She decided to take them under her protection. The older they grew, the dearer they became to her.

At first, she left little gifts for them in some of their favorite places. The fairy took great delight in their innocent enjoyment of finding the little gifts and watching how they would offer them to each other.

Chapter II

When the two children were grown, the fairy resolved to make herself known to the two children. She chose a time when they were sitting in the deep shade of a flowery hedgerow. They were startled, at first, by the sudden appearance of a tall, slender lady, dressed all in green and crowned with a garland of flowers. But then she spoke to them sweetly and told them how she had always loved them.

She said that it was she who had given them all of the little gifts which they delighted in finding. They thanked her gratefully. When she bade them farewell, she told them never to tell anyone else that they had seen her.

"You will see me again," she said. "But, I shall be with you frequently, even when you do not see me." Then, she vanished, leaving them in a state of wonder.

After this, she came often and taught them a number of things. She showed them the marvels of her beautiful kingdom. At last, one day, she said to them, "You know that I have always been kind to you. Now I think it is time you did something for me in turn.

"You both remember the fountain that I call my favorite? Promise me that every morning before the sun rises in the sky, you will go to the fountain and clear away every stone, every dead leaf, and every broken twig that may dirty its waters."

"I shall take it as proof of your gratitude to me if you do not forget nor delay this duty. I promise that as long as the sun's earliest rays find my favorite spring the clearest in all my meadows, you two shall not be parted from one another."

Sylvain and Jocosa willingly undertook this duty. Indeed they felt that it was a very small deed in return for all that the fairy had given and promised to them. So, for a long time, the fountain was tended with the most scrupulous care. It was the clearest in all the countryside.

One spring morning, long before the sun rose, Sylvain and Jocosa were going towards it from opposite directions. Tempted by the beauty of the fields of spring flowers which grew fully on all sides, each one paused to gather some for the other.

"I will make Sylvain a garland," said Jocosa.

"How pretty Jocosa will look in this crown of flowers!" thought Sylvain.

Here and there, they strayed, led farther and farther. For the brightest flowers always seemed just beyond them. Until at last, they were startled by the first bright rays of the rising sun.

At once, they turned and ran towards the fountain, reaching it at the same moment from opposite sides. But to their horror, the usual calm waters now were bubbling. Even as they watched, a mighty stream arose which entirely engulfed the fountain.

Sylvain and Jocosa were parted by the wide, rushing river. All of this happened so quickly that they only had time to utter a cry and for each to hold up to the other the flowers that they had gathered.

Chapter III

Twenty times Sylvain threw himself into the turbulent waters. He hoped to be able to swim to the other side. Each time a strong force drove him back upon the bank to where he started. Jocosa tried to cross the flood on a tree which came floating down torn up by the roots. Her efforts were also useless. Then, with heavy hearts, they set out to follow the course of the stream, which had now grown so wide that they could barely see one another.

Night and day, over mountains and through valleys, they struggled on. They were tired and hungry. They were consoled only by the hope of meeting once again.

Three years passed and, at last, they stood upon the cliffs where the river flowed into the mighty sea. Now they seemed farther apart than ever. In despair, they tried once more to throw themselves into the foaming waves.

The Fairy of the Meadows, who had never stopped watching over them, did not intend that they should be drowned. So, she waved her hand, and immediately they found themselves standing side by side upon the golden sand.

Their joy was tremendous when they realized that their struggle was ended. They felt great happiness as they clasped each other by the hand. They had so much to say that they hardly knew where to begin. But, they agreed in blaming themselves for their lack of attention that had caused their trouble.

When the Fairy heard this, she immediately appeared to them. They threw themselves at her feet and begged her forgiveness. She granted this freely. She promised that now their punishment was ended. She sent for her chariot of green rushes, ornamented with May dewdrops. This carried them all the way back to their home land in a remarkably short time.

Chapter IV

Sylvain and Jocosa were overjoyed to see their beloved home once again after all of their troubles. The Fairy, who was set on securing their happiness, had resolved the conflict between their parents while they were gone. She gained their consent for the marriage of the two.

And, thus, she led them to a charming little cottage, close to the fountain. It once more flowed peacefully down into a little brook which enclosed the garden and a pasture full of sheep.

Indeed, nothing more could have been thought of for Sylvain nor Jocosa. The Fairy had thought of it all. She was quite content to see their delight.

When they had explored and admired it all, they sat down under the rose-covered porch. They listened to the Fairy tell a story while they waited for the wedding guests to arrive.

One day a farmer found an egg, yellow and glittering, in the nest of his goose. When he picked it up, it was quite heavy and he soon discovered, to his delight, it was an egg of pure gold. Every morning he found the same; the goose had laid one pure gold egg. The farmer soon  became rich from selling his eggs. Thinking he would get all of the gold the goose could give at once, he killed the goose and looked inside. Nothing was found.

The Fairy finished her story, and spoke to Sylvain and Jocosa further, "This little cottage and all that belongs to it is a gift more likely to bring you happiness than many things that would at first seem grander. If you faithfully promise me to till your fields and feed your flocks, and keep your word better than you did before, I will see that you never lack anything that is really for your good."

Sylvain and Jocosa gave their faithful promise to the Fairy. Their wedding took place at once with great festivity and rejoicing. They lived to a good old age, always loving one another with all their hearts. Since they kept their promise throughout their lives, they always enjoyed peace and prosperity.

Made in the USA
Middletown, DE
07 July 2015